A DK PUBLISHING BOOK

**Devised by** Claire Watts
**Illustrated by** Graham Corbett

**Editor** Stella Love
**Designer** Adrienne Hutchinson
**Managing Editor** Jane Yorke
**Senior Art Editor** Chris Scollen

First American Edition, 1995
6 8 10 9 7 5

. Published in the United States by
DK Publishing, Inc., 95 Madison Avenue,
New York, New York 10016

A catalog record is available from the Library of Congress.

ISBN 0-7894-0325-0

Reproduced by Bright Arts. Hong Kong
Printed and bound in USA by Inland Press

a b c d e f g h i j k l m

# The Teddy Bear

## A B C

DK

# Aa is for apple, ants, and Adele,

apple

ants

Adele

# B b is for Bruno, butterfly, and bell.

butterfly

Bruno

bell

C c is for Cassie,
crayon, and crumb,

crayon

crumb

Cassie

# D d is for donkey, Dudley, and drum.

donkey

Dudley

drum

**E e** is for elephant, earrings, and Eddie,

elephant

earrings

Eddie

# Ff is for feather, flower, and Freddie.

feather

flower

Freddie

# Gg is for Gertie, goldfish, and glue,

goldfish

Gertie

glue

# Hh is for hat, honey, and Hugh.

hat

honey

Hugh

**I i** is for Ivan,

**J j** is for Jerry,

Ivan

Jerry

# K k

is for koala, kangaroo, and Kerry.

kangaroo

koala

Kerry

# L l is for Luke, lion, and lily,

lion

Luke

lily

# Mm is for mouse, marbles, and Millie.

mouse

marbles

Millie

**N**n is for Norman,
numbers, and net,

numbers

net

Norman

# Oo

is for oranges, owl, and Odette.

oranges

owl

Odette

# P p

is for paint, penguin, and Phil,

paint

penguin

Phil

# Qq is for quilt, Quentin, and quill.

quilt

Quentin

quill

17

# R r is for Rory, rabbit, and rope

Rory

rabbit

rope

**S** **s** is for Sarah,
sand castle, and soap.

sand castle

Sarah

soap

**T**t is for Toby,
trumpet, and thorn,

trumpet

thorn

Toby

# U u is for Ulysses, and unicorn.

unicorn

Ulysses

# V v is for Victor, violin, and veil,

violin

veil

Victor

# W w is for Walter, windmill, and whale.

windmill

Walter

whale

# X x is for Xavier,
# Y y is for Yo,

Xavier

Yo

24

**Z z** is for zipper, Zack, and zero.

zipper

Zak

zero